The search for Blackbeard and his smelly gang of space pirates takes Jake and Moon Granny on a thrilling journey across the stars. However, tracking down the bloodthirsty band of buccaneers is only the beginning. Defeating them is quite another matter.

Saving Great Uncle Raymond and his pet fire newt Flamer will require all of Jake's brains and bravery PLUS the entire contents of Moon Granny's red handbag. But will that be enough? Or will Jake and Moon Granny be forced to walk the plank...in space?

ISBN 9781507618707

The Adventures of

Jake & Moon Granny:

Space Pirate Panic

By Jaye Seymour

About DyslexiAssist™

Part of our mission at Knowonder! Publishing is to make literacy more effective. In order to fulfill that mission for children suffering from dyslexia we are proud to announce our new DyslexiAssist™ initiative: to publish each of our books in a special font designed to make reading easier for dyslexics. You can learn more about it on our website at:

www.knowonder.com/dyslexiassist

When reading with this new font, independent research shows that 84% of dyslexics read faster, 77% read with fewer mistakes, and 76% recommend the font to others who suffer from dyslexia.

Reading stories is a highly enjoyable form of entertainment and learning for many people but people with dyslexia have been unable to find joy from books. We hope this new initiative can now bring the same love and joy of reading to your home!

Thank you to Kathy Rygg and the knowonder! team, and to my family. Particular thanks go to Daniel for his tireless interest, boundless enthusiasm and endless ideas for a sequel.

For Lucy, Daniel and Dafydd

Table of Contents

1

A Surprise Visitor

Jake's grandmother lived a **LONG** way away.

She didn't just live in another town. She didn't live

in a different state or another country. Jake's

Granny didn't even live on the same planet.

All his school friends had kind, cuddly grey-

haired grandmothers whom they saw every week.

They all did nice normal grandmotherly things like baking yummy chocolate cakes and giving out extra pocket money. When the weather turned cold they got out their needles and knitted horrible itchy scarves and jumpers. They came to watch all the school plays and concerts and kept secret supplies of toffees and mints in their handbags.

Jake's Granny never made it to school plays. Living on the Moon made it rather tricky to get there on time. She did keep toffees in her handbag, but her handbag was usually racing around space with her at a zillion miles an hour. And she'd never once knitted Jake a horrible Christmas jumper or a fluffy scarf that made him look like a girl. She just wasn't the knitting type. She'd rather battle aliens

than make pancake batter. She'd rather race

rockets than take walks in the countryside. She was

the coolest, funniest, most exciting Granny in the

whole universe, but Jake wished she lived a little

bit nearer. He could hardly pop in and say a quick

"hello" on his way home from school. His mum and

dad never said, "We're going to Granny's for dinner

tonight, so make sure you put on something clean.

And don't forget to brush your hair. It looks like

you've got a squashed hedgehog stuck to the top of

your head." At least they never said the bit about

dinner.

Jake's parents drove a battered old blue car

with a broken radio and a baseball-shaped dent in the hood. It made an embarrassing grrk grrk grrk sound every time they turned on the engine, like a lion with something stuck in its throat. It was such an old wreck it barely made it to the supermarket and back. Getting all the way to the Moon for dinner and a slice of chocolate cake with Granny was out of the question.

Jake had been working on his own rocket out in the back garden for the past two months but that wasn't going anywhere either. It was made out of three giant crates glued together and sprayed silver, with a neat round window cut out at the front so he could see where he was going. Dad had even fixed up a battery-powered engine and some real flashing lights using a pair of old camping lamps. The end result looked brilliant, but Jake still couldn't get it to start.

He climbed in and tried counting down from ten and shouting "BLAST OFF!" at the top of his voice but nothing happened. When he looked out of the round window he still saw the grass, the apple tree, and the garden shed, not to mention Mum's bottom sticking out of the flowerbed where she was busy pulling up weeds. And, big as it was, Mum's bottom looked nothing like the Moon.

"I know what will cheer you up," Dad said. "It was going to be a surprise but I might as well tell you now. Granny's planning a trip to Earth next

weekend for your birthday."

Jake grinned. "Fantastic! I can't wait!"

Granny's visits were always fun. Adventures seemed

to follow her around wherever she went. Sometimes

she even took Jake with her on a trip into space.

"When is she arriving?"

"Hmm," Dad said, staring thoughtfully up at the

sky. "I thought she said Friday. But it looks like

she might be here a little sooner."

Jake tilted his head back and squinted into the

blue, cloud-wisped sky. It was hard to see anything

against the bright sunlight. But what was that?

There, in the distance, was a tiny silver dot, no bigger than a speck of space dust. As he stared up at it the dot became a small silver spot. He gave a loud whoop of excitement. "Is that Granny?"

"I do believe it is," Dad said.

The spot became a small silver disk.

Dad leapt into action. "Incoming spaceship!" he shouted to Jake's mum. "Speedy Space Gran approaching fast. Clear the garden NOW!"

Mum didn't need to be told twice. She bounded out of the flowerbed and threw her gardening tools into the shed. Dad raced for the washing line, dropping the half-dried sheets into the waiting

basket. He untied the line at the far end of the garden and bundled up the long metal props.

Up through the clouds the small silver disk was becoming a much larger disk. Mum dashed back to the house with the basket full of sheets, muttering crossly under her breath.

"I didn't think she was coming until Friday," she moaned as Dad whizzed by with Jake's football and scooter. "That's typical of your mother, turning up early and expecting us all to be ready and waiting."

"You know what it's like on the Moon," Dad said. "The cell phone reception is terrible."

"Hmmmpphh!" Mum snorted as she helped Jake

drag his rocket across the lawn to safety.

The spaceship was clearly visible now, hurtling through the clouds toward them at a terrific speed. Luckily the old lady who lived next door was away visiting her daughter. Granny's arrivals were very bad for her nerves.

"Quick!" Dad shouted. "Into the house! Grab that cat!"

Jake caught hold of Swish, who came to see what all the fuss was about. He gave a loud meow and dug his claws into Jake's skin to show how irritated he was at having his afternoon snooze interrupted by so much noise and commotion. But

Jake didn't have time to argue with a grumpy cat.

He ignored the pain in his arms and ran toward the

patio door as a round shadow filled the garden.

Phew! They'd made it! Mum pulled the door

shut behind them with a sigh of relief and collapsed

into a nearby chair. Seconds later the gleaming

silver spaceship crash-landed in her freshly weeded

flowerbed.

Jake watched with excitement as the smoke

cleared. Mum stared in horror at what was left of

her poor marigolds and roses. Swish pulled his claws

back out of Jake's arms and jumped down again.

The cat took one look at the spaceship and gave a

big yawn. Evidently it would take more than a silver

ship the size of a small house to interest him. A silver fish the size of a small house would be a different matter. Swish gave another yawn, licked sleepily at his paws, and curled up in his special basket. He was asleep again within seconds, probably dreaming happy cat-dreams of giant silver fish falling from the sky.

Dad squeezed Mum's hand and took a deep breath. "Here she is," he said with a smile.

"Yes." Mum sighed. "Here she is. Right in the middle of my flowerbed as usual."

2

Kidnapped

A square hatch swung open at the bottom of

the spaceship. Out stepped a small, pink-haired lady

dressed in a bright purple space suit.

"Granny!" Jake shouted. He flung the door

open and raced across the garden to meet her.

"Hi, Jakey," Granny said with a grin, scooping him up and whirling him round in the air. "Jumping Jupiter, you're getting heavy!"

Dad rushed out to join them. "Put him down. You'll hurt your back. You're not on the Moon now, Mum."

"I know, I know, the gravity on Earth is much stronger. I remember." Granny smiled. "But don't forget that I'm the third strongest woman on the Moon," she added with a wink.

Jake grinned. "And exactly how many women are there on the Moon, Granny?"

"Only three." She ticked them off on her

fingers. "There's Mrs. Raymore, who's in charge of lighting. Miss Hole, who's in charge of crater cleaning, and me."

Jake waited for her to go on. He loved hearing about her jobs. His friends' grandmothers were all retired now, but Granny wasn't showing any signs of slowing down.

She took a deep breath. "And of course I'm in charge of rocket engineering, alien relations, meteor management, space mail deliveries, data gathering, specimen collection, dust control and, last but not least, cheese tasting. In fact I've brought you all a nice bit of Moon cheese as a treat." She ducked back inside the spaceship. When she came out she was carrying a great round cheesy boulder under one arm. It was covered in shiny purple wax and looked heavy. She handed it to Dad who tried his best to smile.

"There you go," she said. "I know how much you enjoy a slice of Moon cheese in your sandwiches."

"Wow, thanks Mum," Dad said through gritted teeth. He had once told Jake that Moon cheese tasted like sweaty socks mixed with moldy cabbage, but he didn't want to hurt Granny's feelings. "Now, come on in and we'll make you a nice cup of tea."

"Oh lovely," Granny said. "I do miss Earth tea. The stuff they make on the Moon tastes like sweaty cabbage mixed with moldy old socks." She

wrinkled up her nose. "I always have to eat a bit of

cheese afterwards to take the taste away."

"Moldy old socks?" Dad said. "How awful!" He

coughed into his sleeve, and Jake could tell he was

trying not to laugh. "Cabbage and sock-free Earth

tea coming right up," he added, getting out the

best china cups. "Although we weren't expecting

you until Friday."

Granny's face grew serious. "Yes, I know. But

there's been a bit of a change of plan. It's only a

flying visit today I'm afraid."

"What a shame," said Mum under her breath as

she filled the kettle.

"The thing is," Granny went on, "I've had some rather bad news. I wanted to let you know in person."

"What do you mean?" Dad asked. "What's happened?"

Granny took a deep breath. "It's Great Uncle Raymond. He's been kidnapped."

"Kidnapped?" Mum and Dad said together.

Granny nodded. "I'm afraid so. And they've taken poor old Flamer too."

"But who'd want to kidnap them?" Mum asked.

Jake knew she still hadn't forgiven Great Uncle

Raymond for bringing Flamer, his pet fire newt, to

Jake's christening all those years ago. Mum said

that not only had Flamer polished off the cake

while everyone else was in church, he'd also set fire

to her best hat and an entire table full of gifts. By

the time the fire brigade had arrived there was

nothing left except a burnt silver moneybox and a

black, smoking hat.

"Space pirates," Granny said. "The meanest,

smelliest, worst-dressed space pirates in the entire

universe."

Dad let out a shocked gasp and dropped the

best china cups. They smashed into hundreds of

pieces all over the kitchen floor. "You don't mean

Bloodthirsty Blackbeard and his Beastly

Buccaneers?"

"I'm afraid so," Granny said. She held up a

funny little bottle with wings on either side that

made strange cheeping noises. It had a tiny silver

cork in the top. "This arrived first thing this

morning," she said, pulling out the cork.

"Help!" said a man's voice from inside the

bottle. "Flamer and I have been kidnapped by

pirates. Really mean, smelly ones with terrible

fashion sense!"

"And then," Granny continued, "I got a

message from the pirates themselves." She pulled a small silver machine out of her pocket. It was round and shiny with a tiny screen in the middle and buttons on the side. She pressed the top button and a strange picture filled the screen. Jake couldn't figure out what it was supposed to be. It looked like a hairy black cave.

"Is that the pirates' secret hide-out?" he asked Granny. "Is that where they're keeping Great Uncle Raymond?"

"No." She smiled. "It's a close-up of Blackbeard's left nostril."

The nostril on the screen twitched.

"Listen up, Moon Lady," said a gruff voice. "I'm Bloodthirsty Blackbeard the Bad. You've probably heard of me because I'm so mean and scary. And guess what? I've got your brother Raymond here. And I've got his 'orrible lizard thingamabob that breathes fire too. I won't let them go until you pay my beastly buccaneers one million Moon dollars." The nostril twitched again as the pirate laughed. It was a mean, scary kind of laugh. "Bring the money to our pirate ship at...aaaarrrrggghhhh! Get him off! Get that 'orrible fire-newt out of my trousers. Quickly you dozy duffers, before he burns my..."

Then a lady's voice cut in saying, "Message bank is full. You have no more memory available.

Please empty your inbox to create more space.

Thank you."

"Is that it?" Dad asked. "Is that all there is?"

Granny nodded. "My answering machine cut him

off there. I've no idea what the rest of the message

was. I don't even know where they're holding him."

"Have you called the police?" Mum asked. She

was on her hands and knees, sweeping up the broken

china. She gave a long sniff as if she was trying not

to cry. Perhaps the news about Great Uncle

Raymond had upset her. Or maybe it was the loss

of her best tea cups.

Granny rolled her eyes. "You mean the Space

Patrol? They're next to useless. They won't do

anything until they know where Blackbeard's holding

him. So it's down to me I'm afraid. I need to find

out where the message came from."

"How will you do that?" Jake asked. He looked

at the silver machine again. The screen had gone

black.

"First of all," Granny said, "I need to

triangulate the signal."

Jake scratched his head. "What does that

mean?"

Granny shrugged. "I've got no idea. All I know

is that's what they do on Crooks in Space. I'm not

sure you can get it on Earth but it's a great show. Lots of high speed rocket chases. And whenever the baddies leave a message on someone's machine, the detective has to triangulate the signal. He takes it to a mutant hamster in the basement who presses lots of buttons on his computer. And one minute later the hamster knows exactly where the baddies were calling from."

"So where are you going to find a mutant hamster?" Jake asked.

Granny gave a big sigh. "That's the problem. I'm not sure they even exist in real life. But if anyone knows anything about triangulation, it will be the Zabalonians."

"The who?" Mum asked.

"The Zabalonians," repeated Granny. "From the planet Zabalon. Everything's triangular there."

"And green," Dad added. "From what I remember. We went there for the weekend when I was about your age, Jake. They like their triangles and they really like the color green. Oh and they make the best chocolate pudding in the galaxy."

"That's right," Granny said. "It just so happens I have an important package from the Moon Minister to deliver to the King of Zabalon. I'll ask them to triangulate the signal for me while I'm there. With any luck they can tell me exactly where those pesky pirates are. Then it's Moon Granny to the rescue!"

"And where are you going to find the million Moon dollars to pay them?" Mum asked.

"Huh! I'm not." Granny snorted. "Those stinky scoundrels won't get a single cent out of me. They'll be lucky if they can still talk by the time I've finished with them. No one kidnaps my family and gets away with it."

Dad's mouth grew tight and he shook his head. "You can't battle Blackbeard on your own. He's too dangerous. Find out where his ship is and then wait for the Space Patrol. Let them take care of the fighting and action stuff. Okay?" He handed Granny a cup of tea in one of the everyday mugs. "I'd love to come and help with the search but I've got an important meeting at work tomorrow. My boss will go nuts if I miss it."

"I could go," Jake suggested. "I've always wanted to meet a real-life pirate."

"I don't think that's a good idea," Mum told him. "Blackbeard might kidnap you too. Or worse..."

"But it would be an amazing adventure," Jake said.

"Yes." Mum sighed. "That's what I'm afraid of."

Jake guessed she was thinking about his last

'adventure' with Granny—a close encounter with a

volcano on the planet Praxos. The scorch marks on

his boots still hadn't come off.

He had a sudden brainwave. "Don't forget we're

doing a special project on pirates at school. It

would be like doing extra homework!"

Mum raised an eyebrow. She was very keen on

homework.

"Nice try," she said. "But the library is the

place to find out about pirates. Not outer space.

And definitely not face to face with the deadliest

villains in the universe."

Jake tried again. "I wouldn't be face to face

with them. I'd be observing them from a safe distance. And I could always borrow a clothespin for my nose to protect me from the horrible smell."

"I'm sorry," Mum said. "It's still too dangerous. If they can capture an awful fire-breathing creature like Flamer there's no telling what they might do to a defenseless schoolboy."

"But I wouldn't be defenseless," Jake went on. "Mr. Hollix has been running lunchtime karate classes at school. He says I'm really good."

"I'm sure you are." Mum smiled. "But still..."

"We learned a brilliant kick last week," Jake told her. "If it's done right it can bring down a fully grown man." He turned to Dad. "Want me to show you?"

Dad took a step back. "I don't think that will be necessary," he said.

"And I'm an expert on pirate battle tactics," Jake told Mum. "We watched a really cool documentary at school. Granny needs someone like me."

Mum still didn't look convinced, but Jake had one more trick up his sleeve.

"You did say I could do something special for my birthday," he added. "You said I could go wherever I wanted. Well this is what I want to do for my birthday. Please."

Mum gave a big sigh as if she knew when she was beaten.

"Well, maybe if you promise to be really sensible..." she began.

"I do," said Jake. "I do, I do, I do."

"And providing you do exactly what Granny tells you..." added Mum.

"I will, I will!"

"And make sure you come back safe and sound..."

"Of course he will," Granny said. "You have my

word. And once we've rescued Raymond and Flamer we can stop off at Klimra for a bit. How does that sound, Jake? We could visit the Great Pink Lakes and the Firebloom Forest—a few days of swimming and roasting marshmallows on the prettiest planet in the universe. What do you say?"

Jake let out a whoop of excitement and scrambled upstairs to start packing before Mum had another chance to say "no".

"Make sure you bring those green space gloves I sent you for Christmas," Granny called after him. "They won't let you on Zabalon without them."

"And don't forget to brush your hair," Mum

added with a sigh. "It looks like you've got a

squashed hedgehog stuck to the top of your head."

3

Race Against Time

Jake raced around his room, deciding what to

pack. Pirates and chocolate pudding! Pink Lake

swimming and roasted marshmallows in the

Firebloom Forest! This was going to be the most

exciting holiday ever. He fetched his red space

suitcase and threw in a toothbrush and washcloth.

He added an extra T-shirt, his lucky Mutant Space

Snails underwear, his favorite pair of swimming

trunks, and a snorkel and goggles for good measure.

What else would he need?

He found the special space socks Granny had

bought him for their trip to Mars last year, hiding

away at the bottom of his underwear drawer. Mum

hadn't been very impressed with that adventure

either. He stuffed the socks into his case and

smiled to himself, remembering the fun he'd had

with the aliens who'd captured him. He'd been

scared at first, but they were surprisingly friendly

once he'd got to know them. It wasn't their fault

they were giant slug creatures with eighteen pairs

of eyes and long purple tongues. And they hadn't

wanted to eat him or chop him up and feed him to

their pet spiders after all. It turned out they just

needed an extra player for their game of Space

Monopoly.

Jake wondered what the Zabalonians would look

like. Three heads maybe? Yellow spotty wings? He

couldn't wait to find out. But first he needed to

find his green wool space gloves, which were

nowhere to be seen. He emptied out his drawers. He

searched through the washing basket, the linen

closet, and under his desk. But they seemed to

have vanished into thin air.

"Come on, Jakey," Granny called from the bottom of the stairs. "We've got a great uncle to rescue. Who knows what those big, bristly brutes are doing to him? If you don't hurry up, I'm afraid I'll have to go without you."

"No!" he called back, trying to keep the panic out of his voice. "I'm nearly ready. I just need to find my space gloves!"

Clothes and books went flying over Jake's shoulders as his search grew increasingly frantic. Thump! His space atlas crashed against the bedroom door, closely followed by a model rocket. Clatter! A pot of magic markers scattered across the floor. The commotion brought Dad rushing up to help.

Together they emptied out the bookcase and the drawer under Jake's bed. They found a water pistol he'd forgotten he had, a broken yo-yo, and a half-eaten chocolate bar. But no gloves. They found his favorite issue of Mutant Space Snails, a fuzzy brown apple core, and no less than sixteen pencils. But still no gloves. Jake bit his lip, trying not to think about the Firebloom Forest and roasted marshmallows. He tried not to think about strange green planets and Great Pink Lakes. Compared to dashing through space and chasing after pirates, a whole week stuck at home riding his bike and playing on the computer seemed too boring to bear.

Just then Granny appeared in the doorway, clutching what looked like a pair of knitting needles.

"Any luck?" she asked.

Jake shook his head.

"Don't worry," Granny said. "I've had a bit of a brainwave. Your mum's got some bright green wool left over from that horrible jungle jumper she knitted for your cousin Lucy last winter. I'm going to borrow a pair of needles and have a go at knitting you some new gloves on the way. I've been practicing," she added proudly. "After all, isn't knitting things what grannies are supposed to do? The only problem is I might have to leave you in charge of the spaceship for a bit. I don't think I'll be able to knit and steer at the same time. Would that be all right?"

Jake grinned. It was better than all right. It was fantastic! "Do you really mean it? I get to captain the spaceship? Wow!" He paused. "It's not difficult is it?"

"Oh no," Granny said. "It's just like riding a bike. Only with three hundred and seventy-two color-coded buttons and four sets of steering levers instead of handlebars. Oh, and no wheels. But don't worry, I'll talk you through it. Grab your suitcase and say goodbye to your mum and dad. It's time we were off."

Jake kissed his parents goodbye, promising faithfully to brush his teeth, wash his face, keep away from volcanoes, and go to bed at a sensible time.

"And don't get yourself kidnapped by those pirates," Mum added. "As soon as you've found them let the police take over. Remember your 'pleases' and 'thank yous' and don't forget to shake hands politely when you meet the Zabalonians."

"No!" Granny laughed. "Whatever you do, don't try and shake hands with them. They'd be most insulted."

"Really?" Jake said. It all sounded rather

strange.

Granny nodded. "Shaking hands with a Zabalonian is just like spitting at someone here on Earth. In fact they don't even like to look at anyone's hands. That's why we need our trusty space gloves. The politest way to greet a Zabalonian is to raise both elbows and burp loudly."

Mum frowned. "That doesn't sound very polite to me."

No, Jake thought. But it did sound like fun.

"Have a great time," Dad whispered. "And please don't let Granny bring back any more Moon cheese. Mind you, I wouldn't say 'no' to a bit of Zabalonian chocolate pudding."

Mum gave Granny a stern glance. "Make sure you look after Jake," she said, "and fly carefully."

"We will," Granny said. "You don't need to worry about anything. Thank you for the tea and the wool by the way. And sorry about your flowers."

Mum grumbled. "Hmmm. Don't mention it."

She and Dad waited on the patio, waving frantically as Jake and Granny climbed on board.

Jake glanced back one last time to see Swish trotting across the lawn with something clenched between his teeth. Five green wooly fingers dangled

from the cat's mouth and a long piece of unraveled

yarn trailed in the grass behind him.

"Is that one of my...?" Jake began. But he was

too late. Swish and the missing space glove

disappeared over the garden fence and were gone.

4

Meteor Madness

Jake climbed into the black and silver chair

beside the captain's seat and fastened his seatbelt.

"Ready?" Granny smiled, strapping herself in

beside him.

"Ready," Jake said.

"Then off we go. Ten, nine, eight, seven, six, five, four, three, two, one, BLAST OFF!"

There was an explosion of noise and light as they rocketed upward. The spaceship shook wildly. Jake shut his eyes. His head was dizzy and his stomach felt as if it had fallen through the floor. This was always the worst bit.

"Not much longer now!" Granny shouted above the roar of the engines. And then suddenly everything grew still as they reached outer space. Jake opened his eyes again.

"Okay?" Granny asked him.

Jake nodded. Out of the window he saw passing spaceships and distant planets. Somewhere, far below them, lay the Earth. "I think so."

"You look like you could do with some Moonfizz to settle your stomach."

Jake nodded again. "Yes please." Moonfizz was the most deliciously fruity, bubbly drink in the universe. It tasted like strawberries, raspberries, pineapple, and lemon sherbet all fizzed up together. Granny leaned over and pressed a shiny purple button to the far left of the control panel. A round hatch opened near their feet and a thin metal arm shot out with a tray holding a bubbling mug of Moonfizz.

"Now," Granny said, as Jake took a long fizzing gulp of his drink. "Let me show you what you've got to do. Watch carefully. You see this big red button here?"

"Yes," Jake said.

"Well don't ever press that."

"Why not?" he asked. "What does it do?"

"I've no idea. I'm afraid I lost the instruction manual. But I've got a funny feeling that it's something really bad. So whatever you do, don't touch it."

Jake gulped, making a mental note to keep well away from it. "Okay."

"Apart from that it's all very straightforward. This green lever here switches on the auto pilot." She pulled it down into the 'on' position. "That means the spaceship should more or less steer itself. You just need to keep an eye on this screen to make sure we stay on course for Zabalon." She pointed to a funny green planet on the top corner of the screen that looked a little like a cucumber. "This blue button switches on the fog lights, and that yellow one there lowers the meteor deflection shield. The shield will protect the ship if we happen to fly into a meteor storm. You get them around planets sometimes. For little bits of space rock those meteors can do a lot of damage. And that orange button over there is the most important one of all."

"What does it do?" Jake asked.

Granny winked. "It's the radio."

"Right," Jake said, pressing his fingers against the side of his head. "I think I've got that."

"Don't worry," Granny told him, "I'll be right here if you need me. Give me two minutes to fetch the wool and needles and I'll be back to keep an eye on things." She removed her safety belt and floated straight up to the ceiling.

"Whoops!" She giggled. "I forgot to switch the gravity booster on. Can you reach it for me? It's the fourteenth pink button from the left, I think."

Jake counted each button, leaning out of his chair as far as his seatbelt would allow. He stretched out his arm and reached with his fingers. The gravity booster made a slurpy sucking sound as it brought Granny floating back down.

"Thank you," she said. "Why don't you hop into the captain's chair while I get my knitting things?"

Jake didn't need to be asked twice. He unfastened his seatbelt and climbed over into Granny's chair. Captain Jake. He liked the sound of that. He took another long, fizzing gulp of his drink and smiled. Up ahead in the distance he could just make out a pink planet with purple rings round it.

How cool was that? He turned to look out of the

side window. A funny yellow alien with two heads

zoomed past. Both of its yellow mouths were

shouting something and all six of its hands waved

wildly. It pointed to something behind it, but Jake

wasn't sure what. He waved back cheerfully.

"There's a funny two-headed alien outside the

window," he called to Granny who was busy trying

to untangle the green wool from the handle of

Jake's suitcase. "I think it's trying to tell us

something."

A few seconds later Jake found out what that

something was. Bang! Crunk! Boom-boom-boom-

boom-bash! It sounded like someone was firing

rocks against the side of the spaceship. Crack!

Crash! Brilliant bright white flashes flared against

the windshield, almost blinding him. Jake put up his

hand to protect his eyes.

Peering through his fingers, he saw more flaming

lights streaming toward them, bumping and buffeting

into the body of the spaceship. Moonfizz sloshed

over the sides of his mug.

"It's a meteor storm," Granny called as a big

bump sent her flying to the floor. "Quick, Jake,

lower the deflection shield. There's not a moment

to lose!"

"Okay!" he shouted back. He sat up straight in the captain's chair, trying to stay calm. He was in charge now. It was important he got this right.

Hmmm, the meteor deflection shield. Which button was that? He took a deep breath. His hands trembled. Come on, he told himself. You can do this. You just need to remember which color's which. The orange one was the radio, wasn't it? He was pretty certain that was right. And what did the blue one do? That switched on the fog lights....

"Hurry up!" Granny called. "I'm not sure how much more the ship can take!"

BOOOM! Jake was thrown sideways in his seat by an enormous crash. Moonfizz flew across the controls. His seatbelt jerked against his chest, cutting into his arm. It was all he could do to pull himself upright again. His breath came in short frantic gasps. He couldn't even hear what Granny was saying above the battering roar of rocks and space rubble. It was like gunfire—a volley of cannonballs shooting into the metal sides of the ship.

Beads of sweat gathered on Jake's forehead. The yellow one? Was that it? His hand hovered over the row of buttons. No. Don't touch the yellow one. Wasn't that what Granny had said? Whatever you do, don't touch the yellow button. Which just left the red one.

"Here goes nothing," he muttered as the spaceship jerked him sharply to the left. "The red button it is." He straightened up in his seat and pushed down hard with both hands. Either he was about to save the day or blow up the entire ship.

"No!" Granny shouted, pulling herself back up off the floor. "**NOT THE RED BUTTON!**" But it was too late. A terrible wailing noise like a police siren filled the air and all the lights went out.

5

The King of Zabalon

"Jake? Are you okay?"

He could just make out Granny's voice over the

noise of the siren.

"Jakey? Where are you?"

"I'm here, Granny. I'm fine. I'm really sorry. I

got in a muddle."

"Don't worry," she said, "as long as you're safe. Listen Jake, you need to reach under your seat and see if you can find a space lamp."

Jake felt around until he found a small square lamp. He switched it on. There, in a thin beam of light stood Granny. She had a pair of knitting needles and a ball of green wool clutched against her chest.

"Jumping Jupiter!" she said. "I don't know what happened. There's no sign of any more meteors though. We must have passed right through the storm and out the other side."

Jake stared in surprise at the small screen in

front of him. "You're not going to believe this," he said. "We're already there."

"What do you mean?" Granny went to the fuse box and flicked the lights back on.

"We're at Zabalon. Look." He pointed to the screen. The red dot that marked the spaceship hovered over the big cucumber-shaped planet.

"Vaulting Venus! I don't believe it." Granny laughed, looking out the window at the strange bumpy green surface of Zabalon. "That red button must have been the emergency speed transporter. I'd forgotten I even had one. Well done, Captain Jake."

"What about my gloves?"

"Don't worry," Granny said. "We'll just have to put the spaceship onto the hover setting until I get them finished."

Jake sat back in the chair and switched on the radio while she got to work. Space News was just coming to an end.

"And finally we'd like to remind all our listeners to keep a careful eye out for Blackbeard and his gruesome gang of Space Pirates. The bloodthirsty band has carried out a number of attacks across the universe over the last few weeks. They are believed to be armed, dangerous, and very smelly.

Recent reports suggest that some of them also have rather silly looking beards. If you spot the deadly pirate crew, contact the Space Patrol at once on 911111. Then get as far away as possible. Do not attempt to tackle them. I repeat, do not attempt to tackle them..."

Jake tried not to think about Great Uncle Raymond tied up on Blackbeard's ship. What if they hurt him? Smelly pirates sounded bad enough but 'armed and dangerous' ones sounded even worse. The sooner they found the grizzly gang and called the police, the better.

He got himself another Moonfizz and stared out of the window at the rockets and space pods flying past. He spotted a group of blue aliens on cool winged scooters. Then came a long procession of Moon cows and a space farmer in a bright orange tractor pod, which had 'PUTTING THE MOO IN MOON CHEESE' printed across the side. Jake grinned. Perhaps it was the moo that made it taste so bad!

The Venus Vikings tour bus wasn't far behind, with hundreds of concert fan rockets trailing after it. Space traffic was so much more exciting than the cars and trucks on Earth. There was even a giant space wasp buzzing around, closely followed by a SWAT team in its stripy rocket van.

"Finished!" Granny cried after half an hour,

holding up a pair of lumpy green gloves. "They're a bit on the wonky side but I think they'll do."

Jake tried them on. He wasn't going to let Swish get a hold of these. "They're great," he said. "Thanks, Granny."

He climbed back into his own seat, and Granny took over the controls. She had a long gulp of his Moonfizz and then dialed up a number on a silver keyboard. A green creature in a shiny green uniform appeared on the screen. Granny held up her elbows and burped loudly. Jake had to put his hand over his mouth to keep from laughing out loud. Who would have guessed she was such a magnificent belcher?

The creature lifted his shiny arms and burped back. "Greetings," he said. "Welcome to Zabalon."

"Thank you," Granny replied. "I have a package from the Moon Minister to deliver to his Zabalonian Greatness."

"Very good. He is expecting you. And who is the young Earthling?"

"This is my grandson, Jake."

Jake held up his elbows and burped, just like Granny had shown him.

"Hmm, your space gloves are a little lop-sided but I think they will be acceptable. You are welcome here, Jake. You may dock your ship on quay 6078." The creature stuck out his spotty

yellow tongue, nodded twice, and disappeared.

"Okay," Granny said. "Seatbelts on. It's time

to land."

Jake swigged the last of his drink and fastened

his seatbelt. There was a long whoosh of air and a

low hum as the spaceship changed gear. Everything

grew quiet as Granny steered them smoothly down

toward the Zabalonian dockyards and into quay

6078.

Two more uniformed Zabalonians galloped up to

greet them. Jake and Granny stepped out of the

spaceship and burped politely, carrying the big silver

parcel between them.

One of the Zabalonians prodded the package with his gloved fingers. "What's in there?" he asked.

"It's the King's birthday present," Granny explained. "I expect it's a pair of roller skates. The Moon Minister always buys everyone roller skates."

She and Jake were escorted to a funny little car with triangular wheels.

"How can it drive with those?" Jake whispered. "Won't it be really bumpy?"

"They're just for decoration," Granny explained. "You'll see. Come on."

They climbed into the back seat with the package balanced on their knees, and the two Zabalonians got in the front. The driver pressed a big green triangle-shaped button and the whole car lifted up into the air until it floated just above the ground.

"Hold on," Granny warned, "these things are very fast."

She was right. Jake felt like a character in a crazy video game. Whoosh! They zoomed off at top speed, racing out of the dockyard. They sped down a long, green brick road and into the strange green-flowered countryside. Little mint green flowers crept along the ground beneath them. Medium-sized grass-colored flowers with big round petals crowded

along the edges of the lanes. And looking up, Jake

could see towering bottle-green flowers as tall as

trees. Great long drooping petals hung down above

their heads. But there was no time to stop and

admire them. The car raced on toward the capital

city, Zabal, where the King of Zabalon lived.

Granny said he had a great glass palace that looked

like an enormous greenhouse. Jake giggled, picturing

a big cucumber dressed in a cloak and crown.

The car slowed down as they neared the city

walls. The driver pressed the triangle button again

and they came to a halt outside the heavy green

gates. He belched loudly and announced their arrival

to the guard on duty.

"It is the Moon messenger," he said, "and a young Earthling. They have a package for the King."

"Very good," the guard said with a polite burp. The green gates swung open, and they entered the city.

The car dropped back to a lower speed, as if it had run out of turbo boost credits. It glided through the crowded streets. All around them Zabalonians walked, chatted, ate, and shopped. Jake spotted a pet shop with rows of emerald mice in three-sided cages and mint-colored spotted tortoises. Next door a cycle shop sold green bicycles with triangular wheels. A little farther on they passed an outdoor café. A wonderful chocolate fudge smell filled the air.

"Mmm, Zabalonian chocolate pudding," Granny said. She licked her lips. "Perhaps we can come back for some once Raymond and Flamer are safe."

Jake's stomach rumbled just thinking about it. "What about lunch?" he whispered. "I'm getting a bit hungry."

"Leaping light-years, I forgot the Moon cheese sandwiches," Granny said. She pulled a Moonchomp out of her spacesuit pocket. "Will this do for now?"

"Perfect," Jake said. Moonchomps were almost as yummy as Moonfizz. They were soft and biscuity and tasted like apple pie and rhubarb crumble. They had big caramel chips and a soft jelly, custardy middle. He tore off the wrapper and broke it in half.

"No, you eat it all." Granny smiled. "I'll be okay. Besides, we're nearly there now."

Jake finished off the last mouthful as they reached the palace. It looked exactly like Granny had described it, but much bigger and grander. The triangular roof soared up into the sky. This was no ordinary greenhouse. And it was certainly too grand to grow cucumbers in. Even cucumbers in crowns.

The car made a shhhrrrrp sound and sunk back down to the ground. Jake and Granny climbed out and stretched their legs. Royal guards led them through the big glass doorway into an enormous glittering gallery. Green jewels shone in the floor beneath their feet. Sparkling green tiles covered the walls. Jake had never seen such a beautiful room.

"And this is just the entrance hall," Granny whispered as they walked on.

Butterflies tickled the inside of Jake's stomach. He had never met a real life king before. Should he bow or just do an extra loud burp? They entered the dining hall. In the middle of the room sat a huge three-sided table, all set out for a royal feast.

Jake was glad to see that Zabalonian food wasn't all green, unlike everything else on the planet. He couldn't imagine anyone wanting to eat green sandwiches or grass-colored sausages.

They carried on into the grand throne room. A tiny Zabalonian in a glass crown sat cross-legged in a big green armchair. He had a triangular birthday badge pinned to his royal robes.

"Welcome!" The King stood up and presented his elbows to his new visitors. He gave a magnificent belch. "How lovely to meet you again," he told Granny. "I see you have brought me a parcel."

"Yes, Your Royal Greenness," Granny said with a polite little burp. "And I've also brought my grandson, Jake."

"Very good," said the King. "You are most welcome, Your Jakeness."

Jake took a deep breath and gave his best burp ever. It was a whopper. Even Granny looked impressed. All that bubbly Moonfizz had paid off. The King tore at the silver paper on the parcel.

"How kind of the Moon Minister to remember my birthday," he said. "I'm 726 today," he told Jake proudly, pointing to his badge.

Inside was a large silver shoebox. And inside

that was a pair of green roller skates.

"They're perfect," beamed the King. "Just my color. Ha ha! Look at those funny round wheels! Whatever next?" He strapped them on over his shoes and wobbled off.

"Come on," he cried, waving at them to follow. "You must both join me for a spot of birthday lunch."

Granny gave a small bow and chased after him.

"Your Majesty," she said. "I was hoping you could help us with something. My brother, Raymond, has been kidnapped by space pirates. I'm afraid I lost the end of the message so I don't know where

they're holding him. Is there anyone on Zabalon who could triangulate the signal for us?"

"Space pirates?" repeated the King. "How horrid. They kidnapped my auntie once. She said the stench was quite unbearable. We'll do whatever we can to help, dear lady. Send for the royal signalman!"

The signalman was very tall with triangular glasses perched on the end of his nose. Granny handed him the little silver machine and explained about Raymond.

"Ah," he said. "Quite." He rubbed his chin thoughtfully. "Yes. I see. That shouldn't be too much of a problem. Leave it with me."

"And do come and have some lunch while you're waiting." The King beamed. "You can't go chasing off after space pirates on an empty stomach." He led them back into the dining hall. "I believe there's an extra big birthday chocolate pudding for dessert," he whispered to Jake as they took their seats.

The rest of the royal family and the Zabalonian Prime Minister were already there. Jake could hear the soft rumble of hungry tummies round the table as they stared at the delicious-looking mountains of food.

"Jumping Jupiter!" Granny said. "What a spread!"

"Let the feasting begin," the King announced. The guests cheered and filled their plates. Jake helped himself to puffed potato pie from Pluto and ginger gelatin from Jupiter. He tried melon marshmallows from Mercury and nutty nougat from Neptune. Every dish seemed more exciting than the last. There were melted mustard muffins and steaming bowls of mackerel macaroni from Mars. He even tasted some vanilla vegetables from Venus. But they felt all slippery and slimy in his mouth and made his tongue itch. The silver sizzled sausages from Saturn and yellow yams from Uranus were much nicer. It was tricky eating with his gloves on, but he soon got the hang of it.

"I hear you're on a rescue mission," the royal boot maker said. "Nasty lot those pirates. And Blackbeard's gang is the worst. They tried to make a cushion out of my poor old cat."

"That's nothing," the royal pillow fluffer said. "They tried to make a cushion out of my mum."

Jake gulped and set down his sherbet fizzdabber. He wasn't very hungry any more.

"What happened?" he asked. "Is your mum okay?"

"We got her out just in time. She had a lucky

escape, really," the pillow fluffer told him. "Though she was a bit flat afterwards."

"Well I heard they feed their prisoners pickled space slugs," the royal slipper warmer said. "And if they don't do what they're told they make them..."

But Jake never got to hear about Blackbeard's beastly pirate punishments. Just at that moment the royal signalman appeared in the doorway. He gave a loud cough.

"I have triangulated the signal, Your Grand Greenness," he announced with a low bow.

"Very good," the King said. "Where are they then?"

"Well now. It was a little faint after all this time," the signalman went on, "which meant I couldn't get a precise location as such."

The King nodded. "Fair enough. Go on."

"You see the process is a little tricky. It's much harder than it looks on Crooks in Space."

"Yes, yes," the King said with an impatient sigh. "But where are they? Come on, spit it out. It's nearly time for the birthday pudding."

The signalman shrugged. "They're somewhere between Saturn and Uranus. That's all I can tell you I'm afraid."

Granny leapt to her feet. "It's a great start,"

she said. "Thank you so much." She bowed low to the King. "I'm afraid we must leave at once, Your Glorious Greenness. We've got some pilfering pirates to catch. Thank you for everything." She gave a loud farewell burp that echoed round the room. "Come on, Jake!" she called. "To the rescue!"

6

Hunting for Pirates

The King called for a driver to take them back

to their spaceship.

"Thank you again, Your Green Grandness," said

Granny. "I hope you enjoy the rest of your

birthday."

The King sighed. "Such a shame you couldn't

stay for some chocolate pudding," he said. "But maybe next time. Good luck with the pirates, young Jake."

"Thank you." Jake held up his elbows and burped a polite goodbye. Judging by the scary Blackbeard tales he'd heard over lunch, they were going to need all the luck they could get. He climbed into the green hover car beside Granny, and soon they were driving back through the city and out into the countryside.

"They won't hurt him will they?" he asked.

"Hurt who, dear?" Granny seemed lost in thought.

"Great Uncle Raymond. The pirates won't squish him into a cushion or make him eat space slugs will they?"

"Not if I have anything to do with it," she said. Granny had a fierce look in her eye. "I'll teach those reeking rascals to mess with my brother."

Jake couldn't help but smile. Blackbeard and his band of baddies had better watch out.

Back on board the ship, they strapped themselves in and Granny counted down to take-off.

"Ten, nine, eight, seven, six, five, four, three, two, one, BLAST OFF!"

There was a great explosion of noise and light,
just like before. Jake clung to the chair and waited
for the shaking and spinning to stop.

"How are we going to find them?" he asked
Granny when everything grew still again. "There's a
whole lot of space between Saturn and Uranus."

"It's not going to be easy," she agreed. "It'll
be like looking for a needle rocket in a space-stack.
But we'll just have to keep our eyes peeled and
hope for the best. Fingers crossed we get to them
in time."

"So what does a pirate spaceship look like?"

Granny thought for a moment. "It's just like any

other spaceship really," she said. "But it's black with a skull and crossbones painted across the top."

Jake remembered his pirate history lessons from school. "And do modern space pirates sing shanties and wave their cutlasses around? Do they say things like 'Yo, ho, ho, me hearties'?"

"Well I'm not sure about the cutlasses." Granny smiled. "They tend to use laser pistols instead these days. They do still make people walk the plank though. And that's a serious matter in the middle of space. The sooner we save your great uncle the better."

"Why don't we use the emergency speed transporter again?"

"Good thinking, Jakey boy. After all, this is an emergency. We can't leave poor old Raymond to walk the plank, can we?" Granny handed him the space lamp from under her seat. "Okay then. Are you ready?"

Jake tucked the space lamp between his knees and put his hands over his ears. He nodded. Granny pressed the red button, and the wailing siren blared to life. There was a strange bump as the spaceship lurched forward, and for the second time that day all the lights went out.

"Are we there?" Jake asked, his ears still ringing. He flicked on the lamp and pointed it toward the screen.

"We're exactly three hundred million miles away from Saturn," Granny said. "And five hundred and ninety-seven million miles from Uranus. I suppose that's as good a place as any to start looking."

"And when we find the pirate ship—what then?" Jake asked. "Do we just ring the Space Patrol and wait for them to arrest Blackbeard?" It sounded like the perfect plan to him. They could always watch from a safe distance—as far away from the laser pistols as possible.

"Hmm," Granny said. "I'm not sure there'll be time for that." She crossed over to the fuse box and turned the lights back on. "We'll just have to wait and see. But the first job is to find them. We can't do anything until we've tracked them down." She pressed a few more buttons. "There. I've put the ship into auto cruise control. I'll look out on this side and you watch that side."

Jake fetched himself another Moonfizz and swiveled his chair around to the left. Through the window he saw a Saturn to Pluto holiday shuttle bus full of yellow and purple aliens, chugging its way through the solar system. Close behind came an ice-cream rocket van from Venus with its flashing neon 'stop me and buy one' sign. From each of the great speakers along the base of the rocket came a jingly-jangly version of "Twinkle Twinkle Little Star."

"Anything yet?" Granny asked.

"No. Not unless you want to stop for an ice cream."

"Not really. Keep looking."

The afternoon ticked by as they searched. An astro gull flew squawking past. A dish from a broken space probe loomed into view for a moment or two and then was gone again. A lost tourist circled slowly around a comet on his Orbit-100 space scooter. His head was hidden behind an oversized map of the solar system.

Jake wondered what Mum and Dad were doing down on Earth. They were probably busy worrying about Great Uncle Raymond and Flamer. In fact they were probably worrying about him and Granny as well. He wished they could have come too, but Dad had his important meeting and Mum didn't like spaceships. They made her travelsick. And she wasn't very keen on pirates either.

Jake was beginning to think they'd never find Great Uncle Raymond in such a huge expanse of space. Then he spotted something out of the corner of his eye. It was a great ugly black beast of a ship, hovering in the distance like an oversized fly.

"There!" he shouted, pointing out the window. "What's that?"

Granny turned to look. "Catapulting comets! I think you might have found them! Well done, Jakey lad. Let's see if we can get a closer look."

She switched off the cruise control and steered them slowly toward the black ship. Sure enough, there was a large skull and crossbones painted across the roof.

"The Jolly Roger," Granny said under her breath. "Huh! Let's see how jolly you're all feeling by the time I'm finished with you."

Jake gulped. It sounded like she meant business. "Shouldn't we ring the police now?"

"I'm already dialing," she told him, jabbing at numbers '9' and '1' with her finger.

"Hello," said a bored sounding woman's voice through the speakers. "Which service do you require?"

"Police!" Jake shouted. "Send the Emergency Space Patrol at once! Blackbeard and his pillaging pirates have got my Great Uncle Raymond and his pet fire newt!"

"I'm sorry," the voice said. "We are experiencing high levels of crime today. Our patrol teams are all busy at the moment. If you'd like to

leave your details someone will be with you as soon

as possible."

Granny snorted. "We haven't got time for that.

You need to get here NOW."

"If you'd like to leave your details..." repeated

the voice.

"Fine," Granny snapped. She gave their exact

location and hung up. "But we can't just sit around

here waiting," she told Jake. "It might be too late

by the time they finally roll up. It looks like we'll

have to take care of this ourselves."

"What do you mean?" Jake wasn't sure he liked

the sound of that.

Granny stood up. "I mean it's down to us now. We're the only ones who can stop those revolting rotters. Take the controls, Jakey boy."

Jake climbed across to the captain's chair and grasped the bottom steering lever in his trembling hands.

"Are you sure this is a good idea?" he asked, trying to sound brave. What chance did the two of them have against the hairiest scariest villains in the universe?

Granny gave him a big wink. "Ah. I never said it was a good idea. In fact as ideas go it's probably one of my craziest ones yet. A truly bonkers plan.

But they're often the best ones of all. Don't worry,

I won't let them hurt you."

Jake took a deep breath. He could only imagine

what Mum would say if she were here now.

7

Blackbeard On Board

"Okay let's steer her in, Captain," Granny said,

reaching across for the top lever and pulling it

sharply to the left. "It's time we had ourselves a

pirate party."

Jake's stomach turned cartwheels as they came

alongside the black ship. It looked even more

menacing close up. It was shaped like a giant bullet and dotted with yellow lights that glowed like cat eyes in the dark. The metalwork was scratched and dented and the windows had been blacked out. A nasty smell filled the air too, like cheesy feet mixed with rotten fish and banana skins.

"How are we going to get on board?" he asked.

"We're not." Granny smiled. She seemed to be enjoying herself. "We're going to wait for them to come to us."

Sure enough, it wasn't long before they heard the brrreeeep and clunk of the pirates' porta-bridge locking into position against the side of Granny's spaceship. It was followed by a loud knock on the entrance hatch.

"Space pirate," said a gruff voice from the other side. "Let me in, let me in, or I'll toss you in the bin!"

"That doesn't even make sense," Jake whispered.

Granny rolled her eyes. "I'm afraid pirates aren't the cleverest of villains," she said. "At least this one isn't. But that's good news for us. We need to outsmart him if we're going to save Raymond. He's got a laser gun on his side and we've only got knitting needles."

"There is something else we could use as a weapon," Jake said.

Granny smiled as he explained his plan. "It's worth a try," she told him. "Let's do it. Are you ready?"

"Ready," Jake whispered. He took up his position behind the silver fridge where Granny kept her Moon cheese.

"Okay then. Here we go." Granny raised her red handbag high above her head and walked over to the hatch. "I'm just a poor little old lady," she called out. "Please don't hurt me."

"Let me in, old lady," said the voice from the

other side. "If you do exactly what I tell you then no one will get hurt. Well, not too badly anyway. Unless I'm feeling really mean."

"Are you sure about this?" Jake whispered. His heart thumped in his chest. But Granny was already sliding back the lock. She lifted the hatch. A head appeared in the doorway, wearing a black bandana decorated with a white skull and crossbones. Granny signaled to Jake to keep quiet and flattened herself against the wall, waiting.

"Where are you, little old lady?" called the pirate, looking around the spaceship. He was so huge it took him half a minute just to squeeze his shoulders through the hatch. "You're not hiding from nasty old Blackbeard are you? Because I don't like hide and seek. It makes me really grumpy. And you don't want to see me when I'm grumpy."

Jake held his breath. Still Granny didn't move. She waited until Blackbeard had hauled himself all the way on board and then...she pounced. Wham! Jake heard a loud thud and peered around the fridge. Granny had slugged the pirate in the head with her red handbag. Stunned, Blackbeard dropped his laser gun. It fell straight back and skittered across the porta-bridge.

"Oi!" he roared. "What did you do that for?" Blackbeard lunged toward Granny, catching her roughly by the arm. She squealed and dropped her handbag, spilling its contents all over the floor.

"Help!" she screamed. "Quick, Jake. Do something!"

Jake leapt out from behind the fridge as Granny struggled to free her arm from the pirate's grasp. Blackbeard was an ugly-looking brute. A nasty scar ran down his left cheek and his chin was covered in thick grey stubble. Jake caught a fresh whiff of pirate odor as Blackbeard bent down to pick up the ball of green wool that had fallen out of Granny's handbag. Up close he smelled of rotten fish guts and clogged toilets.

"I'll show you what we do with bag-bashing old

biddies," said the pirate as he tried to tie Granny's arms with the wool.

"Get your hands off her," Jake yelled, pinching his nose with his fingers. His voice sounded silly and squeaky.

Blackbeard sneered. "Who are you? Where did you come from?"

There was no time for introductions. Jake thought of Mr. Hollix's karate lessons at school, but suddenly that didn't seem like much of a defense. And he didn't want to risk kicking Granny by mistake. He looked around for something he could use as a weapon against Blackbeard and spotted a can of hair spray at his feet. It must have rolled out of Granny's handbag. He grabbed it and pressed down hard on the button. A thin spray flew right into the villain's face.

"Aaarrgghhh!" he screamed. "My eyes! What have you done? You'll pay for this you little Earth-squeak." Blackbeard lunged toward Jake, reaching for him with his great hairy hands.

Jake's stomach lurched. It might have been from fear or it might have been from the putrid pirate stench. He looked to Granny for help, but she was busy untangling herself from the ball of green wool.

"I'll get you, boy!" growled the pirate. "No one

sprays my eyes and gets away with it. I'll make you walk the plank, you little blighter. I'll squish you like a space banana. I'll chew you up like a melon marshmallow!"

"Granny!" he yelled. "What do I do?"

"I'm all tangled up!" Granny shouted. "You're going to have to run for it!"

Jake didn't need to be told twice. He shot across the spaceship with the angry pirate in hot pursuit.

8

A Sticky Situation

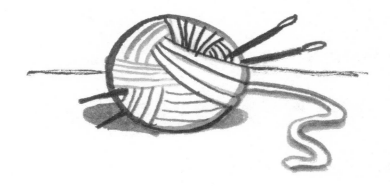

Blackbeard was twice the size of Jake and

twice as slow, but there was nowhere to run on

such a small spaceship. Jake was trapped like a

cornered mouse. And the pirate was like a big

smelly cat, sharpening its claws, ready to pounce.

"Shiver me intergalactic timbers," roared

Blackbeard. "I'm going to make Martian mincemeat out of you, boy!"

Jake ducked back behind the fridge as the pirate lunged for him again. He felt the hot roar of stinky fish breath in his face as he twisted out of the way. The pirate missed by a few inches, stubbing his fingers on the fridge door.

"Ow!" he howled. "I'll get you for that, you sniveling little snot rag. I'll fillet you like a flounder." He sucked at his throbbing red fingers. "I'll roast you like a rack of ribs. I'll have your brains for burgers."

Jake dodged out of the way again, racing over

to the other side of the spaceship. But it was no

good. Blackbeard was hot on his heels. It was only

a matter of time before he caught him.

"Help!" Jake squeaked, with his fingers back

over his nose. "I don't want to be filleted like a

flounder. And I like my brains where they are, thank

you very much!"

"Yarr!" the pirate growled. Perhaps he'd finally

run out of threats. He grabbed at Jake with his

great hairy arms, locking him in a horrible pirate

hug. And this time there was no getting away. Jake

caught a brief glimpse of the tattoo on the pirate's

wrist as the big beefy arms tightened their hold on

him. It looked like a rabbit in a pirate hat, with

117

'Fluffykins Forever' written underneath in bold black letters. That gave him an idea.

"Look!" Jake cried. "Fluffykins has escaped."

"Fluffy?" Blackbeard said, craning his head over Jake's shoulder. He relaxed his hold on Jake just for a moment. "Not my little Fluffy Wuffykins?"

"Here, Jake!" Granny shouted. She had untangled her arms and now held a big bottle of perfume in the air. "Catch!" She flung back her arm and whoosh! The bottle sailed through the air toward him. Jake was impressed. They could use someone like her on his school's baseball team.

Jake forced up his elbows with all his strength,

as if he was greeting a Zabalonian. Ooof! He managed to free one of his arms just in time to catch the perfume. He brought it down with a sharp whack on the pirate's head. There was a horrible cracking sound and the bottle broke clean in two.

"Ro-" Blackbeard stopped in his tracks mid-roar. And then he let go of Jake and crashed backwards onto the floor. Thump! A strong smell of roses filled the spaceship. It was a big improvement on pirate stench.

Jake crawled out from underneath the pirate's legs and brushed himself off.

Granny cheered. "Nice moves. I was hoping a

whiff of old lady perfume might slow him down a bit."

"Well he's not going anywhere in a hurry now." Jake laughed. Blackbeard was out cold.

Granny swept up the broken pieces of glass and handed Jake the ball of wool. "Give me a hand with this," she said. "We need to tie him up before he comes to. Otherwise it'll be Jake-burgers for tea on the pirate ship tonight. With grated Granny garnish!"

Jake lifted up the pirate's big black boots and Granny wound the wool around his ankles. Round

and round it went, binding his feet and legs together tight. Then she did the same to his hands and arms, tying them firmly against the sides of his body. By the time she'd finished, the pirate looked like a big green caterpillar.

"What now?" Jake asked, hoping their part was over. "Do we just wait for the Space Patrol to get here?"

Granny shook her head. "Not while Raymond and Flamer are still in danger." She thought for a moment, and then she smiled. "But now that we've got Blackbeard, I'm sure the other pirates won't be far behind."

Jake shivered. Not more pirates! One had been quite enough.

They sat and waited, keeping a close eye on the big ugly caterpillar in the middle of the floor. He didn't look like he'd be turning into a butterfly anytime soon. But after a few minutes Blackbeard groaned and opened his eyes.

"Ow! My poor aching head!" he moaned. "It feels like someone's walloped me with a dirty great hammer. And what is that terrible flowery smell?"

"It's my best rose perfume," Granny told him crossly. "It was a Christmas present from a very dear friend of mine."

"Then she must be a friend with no sense of smell," Blackbeard said. "Pooh, what a pong!"

Granny looked a little hurt. "That's rich, coming from a whiffy old whiffster like you." She unwrapped a toffee that had fallen out of her handbag and popped it into the pirate's mouth. He chewed it slowly for a bit and then his mouth stopped.

"Eow," he said, "oov uck eye eef ooever."

"What?" Jake asked.

"I ed oov uck eye eef ooever," Blackbeard repeated.

Jake shrugged. "I can't understand what you're

saying."

"I think," Granny said, "he's trying to tell us that we've stuck his teeth together. The old sticky toffee trick! It works every time. Not so scary now, are you, my pirate friend? Thought you could take on a little old lady and her grandson and get away with it, did you?" She waved her finger at him and tutted. "You ought to be ashamed of yourself."

Blackbeard sneered.

"What about my Great Uncle Raymond and his fire newt?" Jake asked. "Did you kidnap them?"

Blackbeard scowled.

"And you thought we'd pay you one million

Moon dollars to get them back?" Granny asked. "And I suppose if we didn't cooperate you were going to make them walk the plank?"

Blackbeard let out a low growl.

Just at that moment there was another burst of banging on the entrance hatch.

"Are you in there, Blackbeard?" shouted a voice.

Jake stared at the pirate's stubbly chin. "I hope you don't mind me saying, but Blackbeard's a funny name for a pirate with no beard."

"I oosed oo ave a ig ack eard ut I aved it off en it arted oing ay." The pirate's jaws were getting a little looser now after some serious sucking on the toffee, but it was still rather tricky to work out what he was saying.

"You used to have a pig-waxed ear but you saved a moth when it farted going away?" Jake puzzled.

The pirate rolled his eyes and shook his head.

Jake tried again. "You used to have a big rack of beer but you waved your glove when it started snowing in May?"

Granny smiled. "I think he's trying to say that he used to have a big black beard but he shaved it off when he started going grey."

The pirate nodded. "Es," he said. "At's ight."

"Blackbeard!" came another shout from outside.

"Ey've ied ee up an uck eye eeth ooether ith o-ee," Blackbeard cried.

"What?" bellowed the voice. "They've got wide tea cups and sucked dry beef shoe leather with coffee? That sounds disgusting."

Granny picked up the can of hairspray and crossed back over to the hatch.

"He said," she called through the door, "that we've tied him up and stuck his teeth together with toffee. If you want him back in one piece you need to hand over your prisoners, Raymond and Flamer."

"With pleasure," said the voice. "That bloomin'
fire newt's been nothing but trouble. He's burnt a
hole in my best trousers and singed Long John
Mercury's beard right off. Worst prisoners we've
ever had, those two. Tried to make them walk the
plank but that newt burnt it clean away."

"So you'll hand them over, just like that?"
Granny asked. "This isn't some kind of sneaky trick
is it?"

"Pirate's honor," said the voice. "Open up this
hatch and we can swap prisoners."

"Okay. But I'm warning you. No funny business.
I've got my trusty hairspray at the ready."

"I'll send for them now," the voice said. "Fetch the prisoners!"

"Aye aye skipper," someone on the pirate ship called back.

Jake watched through the window as a plump pirate in orange spotty trousers appeared on the porta-bridge, dragging Raymond behind him. Jake recognized his great uncle at once from the christening photo album. And the funny-looking red creature draped across Raymond's shoulders must be Flamer. There weren't any pictures of the fire newt in the photo album, just a few close-up shots of Mum's burnt hat. Another pirate in a torn yellow T-shirt brought up the rear, hurrying everyone across the bridge toward Granny's spaceship with a wild wave of his laser gun.

"Raymond!" Granny cried, flinging open the entrance hatch. "You're all right! They didn't hurt you?"

"No." Great Uncle Raymond smiled. "Flamer looked after me, didn't you fella?"

The fire newt bared his teeth and rings of smoke came out of his ears.

"That's enough chit chat," the pirate in the yellow T-shirt said. "What have you done with Blackbeard? Bring him out where we can see him. You can have your pesky prisoners back once we know he's all right."

Jake fetched Blackbeard a glass of Moonfizz to wash away the toffee. And then he rather wished he hadn't.

"Why you moldy little maggot," Blackbeard roared as soon as he could speak again. "You dirty dollop of dingbat droppings. You untie me at once, d'you hear? Or I'll pummel you flat like a Pluto pear pancake. I'll skin you like a stinky Saturn slipperfish."

"There'll be no pummeling, thank you very much," said Granny. "And certainly no skinning. You apologize to my grandson, you big brute, or I'll get my knitting needles on you."

"The only thing I'm sorry for is not squishing the pair of you when I had the chance," Blackbeard snarled.

"Huh!" Granny said, shaking her head in disgust. She and Jake helped him up onto his feet. He hopped across to the hatch and peered out.

"I'm fine," he told his comrades. "Apart from an aching head. And a sore jaw. And horrible stingy eyes. I might have to get one of those black patches. In fact I might need two!"

"I think that was my fault—from the hairspray," Jake said. "Er, sorry."

"Sorry?" roared Blackbeard. "Sorry! I'll give you bloomin' sorry. Why, I'll crush you like a..." he began to say, until he saw Granny raise the can of hairspray. "Let's get this over with," he growled. "I need to get back and check on Fluffykins. Have you seen him? Is he all right?"

"I thought you had him," said the pirate with the yellow T-shirt. "His hutch is empty."

Blackbeard gasped. "You mean it's true? He really has escaped? Then what are you waiting for? Lose the prisoners and let's get out of here. I want all hands on deck to scour my ship until we find him!"

The pirates untied Raymond, and he and Flamer climbed on board Granny's spaceship.

"Good riddance," said the pirate with the orange spotty trousers. He rubbed his pink-looking chin. "It'll take me years to grow another beard as long as that."

Granny and Jake pushed the wool-wrapped Blackbeard out through the hatch, and his crew helped him back to the pirate ship.

"And good riddance to you too," Granny said. She closed the hatch with a big sigh as the porta-bridge slid back into its metal casing below the skull and crossbones. "I could do with a nice cup of tea after that," she added. "A proper Earth cup, not that horrible stuff we drink on the Moon."

"No time for that now," Jake said, pulling the spare passenger seat out for Raymond. "Let's get out of here before the pirates change their mind."

9

Homeward Bound

Granny's spaceship sped off in one direction and

the pirate ship roared off in the other. Ten minutes

later the Space Patrol rocket raced past, its sirens

blaring.

"Better late than never, I suppose," Jake said.

"But the pirates will be thousands of miles away by

now. The police will never catch them."

"You're probably right," Granny agreed. "Still, I think that's the last we'll see of Blackbeard and his crew. I wonder where his precious rabbit got to?" She turned to Great Uncle Raymond who had gone rather red in the face and wouldn't meet her gaze. "Now then, what about your spacecraft? Where did you leave it?"

"It's at the garage," Raymond answered, "getting its brakes fixed. We had to take a space taxi to Uranus and back."

"Were you on holiday?" Jake asked. "Is it nice at this time of year?"

"No, I had to take Flamer to the vet. Poor old thing's got a nasty cough. But we never made it that far, thanks to those pesky pirates."

Flamer coughed and a sheet of flame shot across the spaceship. Jake's green gloves were reduced to a pile of smoking ash.

"Oh dear," Raymond said. "He seems to be getting worse." He patted the large front pocket in his space-coat. "And the pirates took all my money—I'll never afford the vet's bill now. You know how expensive everything is on Uranus."

Jake had a brainwave. "Dad took our cat Swish to our local vet when he broke his leg. The vet did

a really good job, and I don't think she charges too much. You could take Flamer there."

Flamer coughed again and burnt a hole right through Granny's red handbag.

"That's a good idea," she said. "But what about our trip to Klimra, the Great Pink Lakes, and the Firebloom Forest? I was going to show you the sights. And don't you want to go back to Zabalon to pick up some chocolate pudding?"

Jake smiled. "That's okay, Granny. I think I've probably seen enough today to last a whole year! Besides, they won't let me back on Zabalon with burnt space gloves. And you haven't got any more wool to knit me another pair."

"It's a very kind offer," Raymond said. "But what about your mum and dad?"

"They'd love to see you again," Jake told him, trying not to think about the look on Mum's face when she saw Flamer. "You and Granny could stay for my birthday and have a little holiday on Earth." Hopefully Mum would come around to the idea. Eventually. And in the meantime he'd just have to keep the fire newt out of her way. He and his friends could take him for walks in the park. Just so long as Flamer didn't start coughing at the ducks.

Raymond grinned. "It does sound nice. Your dad

and I can catch up on some proper uncle-nephew

time together, as long as you're quite sure your

mum won't mind."

Granny gave Jake a mischievous wink. "She'd be

only too happy to see you again. She's always

saying how lovely it was when you and Flamer came

to Jake's christening."

"Then that's settled," Raymond said. "A bit of

fresh Earth air will probably do Flamer a world of

good."

10

The Stowaway

Everyone was in a holiday mood on the journey

back to Earth. Raymond had some melon

marshmallows and a packet of silver Saturn

sausages, which Flamer kindly sizzled for them.

Granny put the radio on, and they all took turns

driving the spaceship. Jake was starting to get the

hang of it now and couldn't wait to tell Mum and

Dad about his new skills when they got back home.

They fastened their seatbelts as they neared Earth,

and Granny took the controls, ready for the final

landing.

Jake watched through the window as they

approached his house. He saw his parents relaxing

with a cup of tea in the garden until they spotted

the ship hurtling toward them for the second time

that day. They sprang into action, sprinting back to

the house, still clutching their cups. Swish the cat

raced up the nearest tree. Moments later the

spaceship landed with a loud crash in Mum's freshly

replanted flowerbed.

Oops, thought Jake. She's not going to be happy about that.

Mum and Dad were already waiting for them on the lawn by the time Granny and Jake emerged through the hatch.

"Here they are," Dad said with a big smile.

Mum's smile disappeared when she caught sight of Raymond and Flamer. "And I see they've brought your uncle and that horrible fiery creature with them," she said. "Oh joy."

Swish came down from his tree and sniffed at Raymond's coat pocket, which wriggled and squirmed in a most alarming manner. Jake guessed it was full of space worms for Flamer, but he was too excited about his trip to give it another thought.

"Guess what?" he said. "I got to steer the spaceship and we had lunch with the King of Zabalon and escaped from a meteor storm and tied up a scary space pirate and..."

"Whoa, slow down," Mum told him. "Did you say you tied up a space pirate?" She gave Granny a stern look.

"Don't worry," Granny said. "We won't be seeing them again. No more space pirates for us, eh Jake?"

Raymond coughed as something jumped down

from his coat, and Swish gave a loud meow. Jake

stared in amazement as a fluffy white rabbit in a

tiny pirate hat bounded off across the grass with

Swish in hot pursuit.

"Is that Fluffykins?" he asked. The rabbit made

an impressive dive for Mum's watering can and lay

cowering inside, just out of reach.

Raymond coughed again and stared at his feet.

"Yes," he said.

"And how did he get here?" Granny asked in

her sternest voice.

"Well they had my Flamer," Raymond said. "I

thought if I took Blackbeard's precious rabbit we

might be able to swap." He took out a yellow handkerchief with a big scorch hole through the middle and wiped his forehead. "I was going to give him back, honestly, but then it was too late..."

"We'll just have to hope Blackbeard doesn't come looking for him," Granny said. But then she smiled. "At least we've got you and Flamer back safe and sound. That's the main thing." She turned to Jake. "It's been quite a day, hasn't it?"

"Why don't you tell us all about it over a cup of tea and a nice slice of Zabalonian chocolate pudding?" Dad suggested, picking up the watering can with the rabbit still inside. "And then we'll see about turning your homemade rocket into a rabbit hutch for Fluffykins."

Jake frowned. "I'm afraid there wasn't time to buy any pudding in the end. We were in such a rush to rescue Great Uncle Raymond..."

Granny patted Dad's arm. "But don't worry," she said. "I've got another Moon cheese you can have instead."

"Lovely," Dad groaned as they all went inside. "My favorite."

About The Author

Jaye Seymour is a Cambridge University English graduate and previous winner of the Commonwealth Short Story Competition. Her fiction has appeared in a number of publications on both sides of the Atlantic, including The Guardian, Mslexia, The First Line, Short Fiction and Knowonder! She was shortlisted for the 2013 Greenhouse Funny Prize and lives in Devon, England.

About Knowonder!

Knowonder is a leading publisher of engaging, daily content that drives literacy—the most important factor in a child's success.

Parents and educators use Knowonder tools and content to promote reading, creativity, and thinking skills in children from ages 0–12.

Knowonder's storybook collections and chapter books deliver original, compelling new stories every day, creating an opportunity for parents to connect to their children in ways that significantly improve their children's success.

Ultimately, Knowonder's mission is to eradicate illiteracy and improve education success through content that is affordable, accessible, and effective.

Learn more at www.knowonder.com

Made in the USA
Lexington, KY
14 December 2016